PARI NEEDS A MOBILITY AID

Written by Iffat Damji
Illustrated by Richelle Watson

"Be true to yourself and accept yourself as you are."

Pari Needs a Mobility Aid

Written by

Iffat Damji

Illustrated by

Richelle Watson

<u>Dedication</u>

This book is dedicated to my parents who
Have always supported me and never left my
Side even through the tough times.

To my former therapist, Sofana Kassam,
Who encouraged me to pursue my dreams
and in turn inspired me to write this book.

To the disabled and chronically ill
Community on Twitter (Now X), thank you
For accepting me and allowing me into your
community.

To my inner child, that you may never feel
Alone again.

To any children out there who feel like they
Don't belong, "fit" in or that they
Are "not normal". You belong here and there is no such
thing as normal.

There once was a girl named Pari
who wanted to dance and play but one day
she started to realize that she wasn't
like her other friends.

She was always exhausted, in pain and had
trouble walking and she didn't know who to tell.
So she just keptgoing and hoped
it would get better on its own.
But it didn't so she told her mother
and father that she wanted to go to the
doctor, that something wasn't right.

The doctor said "how can I help you?"
and proceeded to do some tests on Pari.
Pari was quite nervous as she didn't know
what the doctor would say.
As days went by, the doctor discovered that
Pari not only had scoliosis but she
had sciatica and dysautonomia too.

The doctor said "no wonder you are always
so tired and I'm glad that you listened to your
body and came to me as soon as you knew.
But you will have to take medication and
possibly use a mobility aid as well."
Pari's parents did not like what
the doctor had said. Their daughter was only
10 years old and besides what will people say?

Pari felt so confused by her parents' reaction.
Was she supposed to feel embarrassed
because she had a chronic illness/disability
at her "young" age?
Were mobility aids only supposed to
be for elderly people? I
mean those are the only people
she saw using them.

She had so many questions but didn't know where she would find her answers.
So Pari and her parents proceeded to drive home in silence. No one knew what to say to one another. They were all so shocked and confused.

A few days later, Pari's parents convinced her to visit their local mosque to search for answers from God.

That is when she saw this beautiful young lady with luscious brown hair wearing a pink anarkali suit, gold flats, jhumka earrings and a bindi using a walker.

Amazed by this woman, Pari decided to approach her. She asked
the young lady what her name was.
The young lady replied "My name is Rani.
What is your name?"

Before Pari could respond, she noticed
that all of the worshippers were looking at this
young lady as if she was an alien, something
they have never seen before, something unusual.
They were whispering amongst one another
about her but Rani didn't seem to care.

Pari told her, her name and then proceeded
to ask her a question.
"If you don't mind me asking, doesn't it upset
you that people look at you this way? Don't you
feel embarrassed or ashamed that you
have to use a walker at such a young age?

Rani chuckled a little and replied "Who told you that you have to be a certain age to use a walker?" Pari didn't really know who taught her this but she never saw a young person using one up until this point.

Pari continued to tell Rani what the doctor had told her and her parents about Pari needing to not only take medication but also that she would potentially have to use a mobility aid.

Rani sat down and let out an exhale. She said "You know Pari, I too was like you, I thought that taking medication was a "bad" thing and that using a mobility aid was only for elderly people.

Even though no one directly told us these things, somehow along the way we learned them and began to believe them.

It took a long time for me to accept
that I needed to use this walker as well and
for a while I was quite embarrassed and
ashamed to even leave my house with it
because I was afraid of what people
would say.

But you know what Pari, it doesn't matter what people think, the only opinion that matters is your own. So if in your heart you feel that your life will be easier and better using one then why not take that chance?"

"I'll tell you one thing, I've never felt more free since I made the choice to use my walker. I can breathe better, I'm not as tired or in pain as I used to be and it feels like I'm living life again. Doesn't that sound amazing?!"

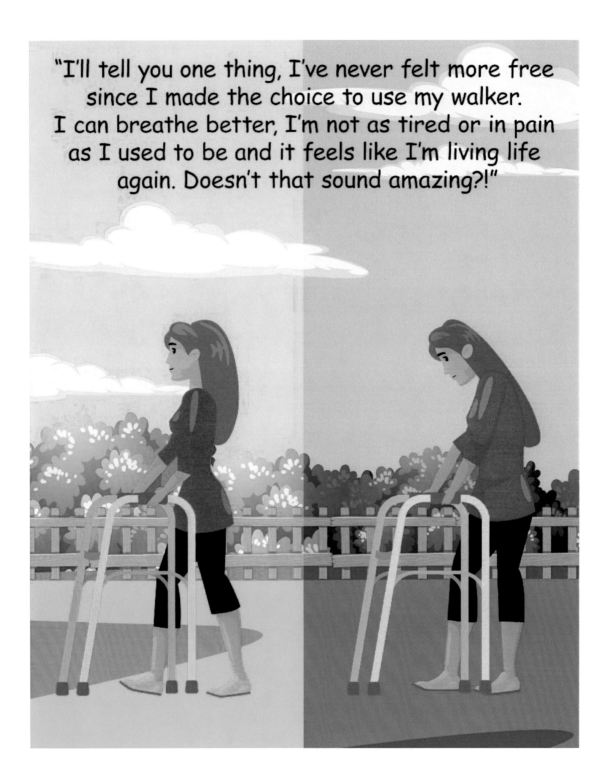

Pari smiled and said "Yes didi (sister) that sounds wonderful! Thank you for all your help." Rani smiled, placed her hand under Pari's chin and said "You are so welcome my dear, please take care of yourself." And they both parted ways and went inside the prayer hall to pray.

Later that evening, Pari told her parents about Rani and how she accepted that she had to use a mobility aid because she could not suffer anymore.

Pari said "Mummy, Papa, if using a cane, wheelchair or walker can make my life easier then why should I not give it a chance? Who cares what people think!" With a bit of hesitation, Pari's mother and father replied "Okay beti (daughter) we will give it a try and see."

So the next day, Pari (with the permission of her parents of course) went online to search for a cane. She came across a sparkly blue one and then asked her father if he could purchase it for her.

Her father said" Sure mera bacha (my child), it looks perfect for you." A few days later, a package arrived in the mail.

It was Pari's cane! Pari and her parents
opened the box and assembled the
cane. Then Pari began using it.

At first, Pari was stumbling a little, it felt weird for her but as the days went on and she had more practice, she got better at using it.

On one Friday evening, Pari decided that she was feeling a bit better and wanted to attend Friday prayers at her local masjid (mosque). At first, Pari's parents were hesitant because they weren't sure how people would react to their daughter using a cane at the age of 10.

They also weren't sure how Pari would feel. As soon as they reached the parking lot and Pari stepped out with her cane, a couple of aunties and uncles started looking and whispering to one another.

One of the aunties approached Pari's parents and started yelling "What is wrong with your daughter? Aren't you embarrassed and ashamed of letting her come out like this?!"

To which Pari's mother responded "There is nothing wrong with my daughter but rather there seems to be something wrong with your outdated way of thinking."

Pari's father added that he and his wife were proud of their daughter as she has overcome so many challenges that life has thrown her way.

They love and accept their daughter no matter what and they will continue to support her decisions if she believes they are right for her.

And they don't care what anyone has to say! Pari heard everything that her parents said and she smirked.

Pari and her parents continued to walk into the prayer hall standing proudly as the sun set behind them.

About The Author

Iffat Damji is a disabled/chronically ill writer. She suffers from long COVID, inappropriate sinus tachycardia (a form of dysautonomia), unexplained seizures, scoliosis, and sciatica amongst other ailments that make daily living difficult. Despite this, she has continued to pursue her writing career. In fact, one of her poems has been published in a book entitled Nectar by Polar Expressions Publishing. She also has her own blog Empathetic Advocate where she discusses issues relating to international development and advocay

About The Creative Minds Behind This Book.

This book was illustrated by two illustrators. The first illustrator, Andrea Milan did the illustrations in the beginning. You can find her on X, her account name is @Drea_milannn

Richelle Watson is the second artist behind the illustrations in this book and the one to finish them. She is a dynamic illustrator and also assists as an editor. She graduated from Chicago State University with a Bachelor's of Art and Design. She is a passionate freelancer from Chicago. Over the years, she has worked on a variety of book projects. She is the second artist behind the illustrations in this book and the only one to finish them. She has an understanding of creating book visuals that stand out from the rest.
Her goal is to assist authors in capturing the narrative through
stunning visuals that will allow readers to fully immerse themselves
in the story.

You can reach out to her via her email, which is richellewatson90@gmail.com